cook's kitchen reference

ONIONS